MINDBENDERS

SCIENCE TRICKS

COMPILED BY
NORMAN BARRETT

Kingfisher Books

Kingfisher Books, Grisewood & Dempsey Ltd
Elsley House, 24-30 Great Titchfield Street, London W1P 7AD

First published in 1992 by Kingfisher Books
10 9 8 7 6 5 4 3 2 1

British Library Cataloguing in Publication Data
A catalogue record of this book is available from the British Library.

ISBN 0 86272 907 6

Editor : John Grisewood
Design : Mustafa Sidki
Cover Design : Terry Woodley

Printed and bound in Hong Kong

Cover Illustration : How water bends light. Light rays
change direction when they enter water and make the
straws look as if they are bent in the middle

CONTENTS

1 THE MIGHTY ATOM

Everything is made up of tiny particles called atoms. They are so small that we cannot see them, even with a microscope. The tiniest speck we can see under an ordinary microscope has more than 10 billion atoms.

There are different kinds of atoms, and they make up all the substances we know.

A substance made up of only one kind of atom is called an element. Iron and gold, both metals, are elements. So is oxygen, a gas. There are more than 100 elements.

Most substances are made up of more than one element. They are called compounds. Water is a compound. It is made up of hydrogen and oxygen.

It's elementary

All the elements have symbols, often their initial letter. Oxygen's symbol is O, for example, and hydrogen's H. The letter I is used for iodine, but what about iron? Do you know what it is? (A clue – it comes from 'ferrum', the Latin word for iron.)

Inside an atom

Small as it is, an atom is not the smallest particle. An atom is made up of even tinier particles. At its centre, or 'nucleus', are a cluster of particles called neutrons and protons. Other particles, called electrons – and this is the difficult part to imagine – whirl at amazing speeds through empty space around the nucleus.

Each element has a different number of protons. Hydrogen has 1 proton, for example, and iron has 26.

Here's some more 'inside information' for you. Protons and neutrons are roughly the same size and nearly 2,000 times as heavy as electrons. An atom is about 100,000 times as big as a proton.

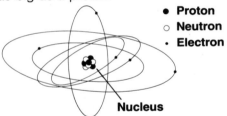

- • Proton
- ○ Neutron
- · Electron

Nucleus

Solids, liquids and gases

Substances are either solids, liquids or gases. Some can be all three. If you freeze water, it becomes a solid – ice. If you boil it, it becomes a gas – steam.

In a solid, the atoms are arranged in a certain pattern and cannot move. In a liquid, they are free to move, but stay close because they are attracted to each other. In gases, they are far apart and move around at high speed.

What is each of these substances, solid, liquid or gas: wood, steel, carbon dioxide, chocolate, milk, mercury, copper, air?

Chocolate

Air

Milk

Odd one out

Can you say which is the odd one out in each of these groups and why?

(1) Gold
    Carbon
    Water
    Oxygen
    Nitrogen

(2) Gold
    Silver
    Iron
    Bronze
    Copper

(3) Gold
    Sulphur
    Nickel
    Brass
    Zinc

(4) Air
    Hydrogen
    Nitrogen
    Methane
    Silicon

(5)

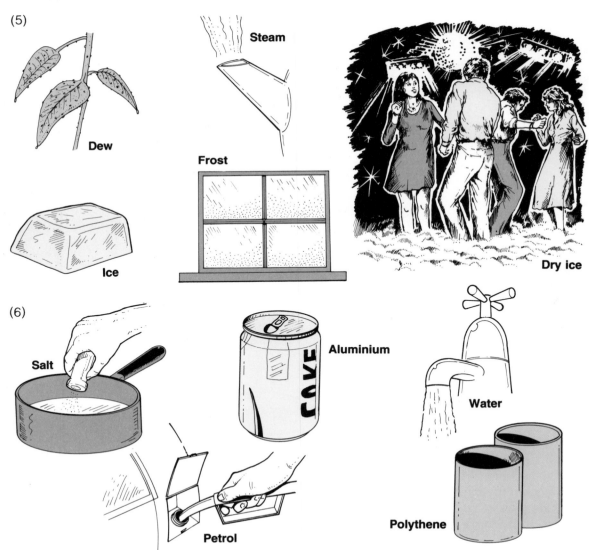

Dew

Steam

Frost

Ice

Dry ice

(6)

Salt

Aluminium

Water

Petrol

Polythene

2 ALL ABOUT AIR

Air is all around you. But it is difficult to think about because you cannot normally see, taste, smell or touch it. But you can feel air when it moves, as with the wind on your face. You can see it, too, if you look at air bubbles underwater. And air carries the smells of other things, such as the scent of flowers or the fumes from petrol.

Weighing air

Weighing air might sound like a job for the scientists, but you can do it yourself quite easily. Set up a simple balance with a stick, a flat-sided pencil and a couple of cans as in the illustration. Use sticky tape to attach an empty balloon at each end, and make sure the stick stays level. This means that the balloons weigh the same.

Mark the stick where it rests on the pencil before removing one of the balloons and blowing it up with as much air as you can. Now fix it back to the end of the stick, making sure your mark is still over the pencil. The balloon will now make the stick dip down. This shows it is heavier now that you have filled it with air.

About how much do you think the air in a large room in your house would weigh:

1 gram, 1 kg, 7 kg or 70 kg ?

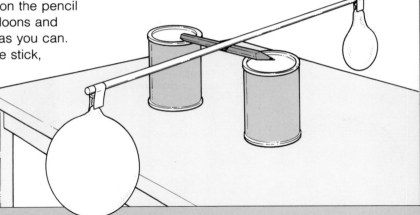

Bottles of air

Fill a bottle with air. On second thoughts, don't bother, just take an 'empty' bottle – it will be full of air already. Push it underwater and watch the bubbles come to the surface. They are the air from the bottle as it fills with water.

What happens if you hold the bottle upright in the water? The air stays in, as in the drawing on the far right. As water begins to enter the neck of the bottle, it is held back by the air, so the water can't get in.

 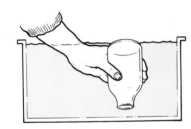

A lot of hot air

Warm air is lighter than cold air. So air rises as it gets warm and cold air moves in to take its place. This causes currents of air to move around, outdoors as well as indoors. A hot-air balloon has a gas-burner to heat the air inside it and make it rise.

Hot air takes up more space than cold air. You can prove this for yourself by fitting a balloon over the neck of a bottle. Now stand the bottle in a bowl of hot water. Soon the balloon will start to inflate. This is because the air in the bottle is heated by the water and expands. Empty out the water and surround the bottle with ice. As the air is cooled, it contracts and the balloon goes down again.

Hot water

Ice

Air to keep you warm

Warm things cool down fast if they are left in cold air, as everybody knows. Heat travels away from the warm objects into the cold air.

Here's an experiment you could try if you had four similar jars and a thermometer. Remove the lids from the jars and wrap them up as shown in the illustration – (1) in a box with loose newspaper around it, (2) with newspaper wrapped round and held in place with elastic bands, (3) loosely wrapped in a scarf or blanket, and (4) with no wrapping.

Fill the jars with hot water, quickly replacing the lids and covering the tops in the same way. Leave the jars in a cool room and after about half an hour take the temperature of each one with a thermometer.

Which jar do you think contains the warmest water?

Several layers of clothing will keep you warmer than one item of thick clothing – true or false?

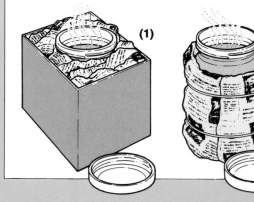

(1)

(2)

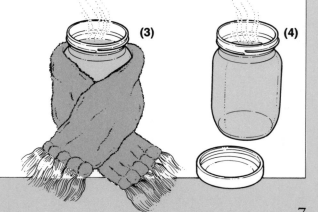

(3)

(4)

Air pressure

When you swim underwater you can feel water pushing on your body. The air around you does the same, but your body is used to it so you do not even notice. The pressure is caused by a layer of air, called the 'atmosphere', which surrounds the earth.

Do you know how much air presses down on every square centimetre of your skin? Is it 1 gram, 100 g, 1 kg or 10 kg ?

The power of air

Here's a trick to show how powerful air pressure is. Place a ruler on a flat table so that about a third of it sticks over the edge. Spread a large piece of paper – newspaper will do – over the table, right to the edge so that it covers the part of the ruler on the table. Now hit the ruler and try to make the paper fly into the air.

You will find this is impossible. In fact, you must be careful not to hit the ruler too hard, or you will snap it! This is because the paper has a large area, so there is a lot of air pushing down on it.

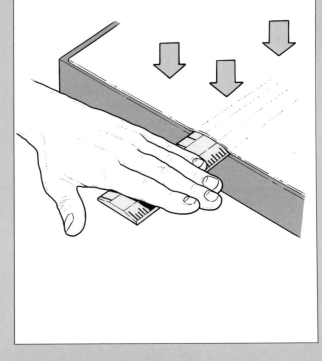

The magic glass

This is a great trick, but practise it first before you show anyone else. You will need a glass with a smooth rim and a piece of smooth card – a postcard will do. Perform the trick over a sink or bowl, so that if anything goes wrong you won't make a mess all over the place.

Fill the glass right up to the top with water and wet the rim slightly. Place the card on top of the glass. Holding the card firmly in place, turn the glass over. Now take your hand away from the card.

The water should stay in the glass! Don't give up if this doesn't work first time. Try again, perhaps with a bigger card. The trick works because of the pushing power of air against the card. It is greater than the downward force of the water.

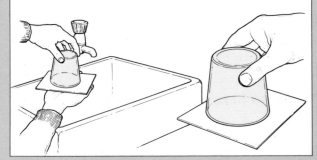

Air on the move

When air moves, it does not press on objects with as much power as still air. Objects might look as if they are being sucked into a stream of moving air, but really they are being pushed into the air stream by the stronger pressure of the other air around them. There are some very simple experiments you can do to show this.

First, hang up two apples about 5 cm apart. Blow between them and try to separate them. Can you do it? No. You will be surprised, perhaps, to find that they move closer together. This is because, by blowing, you move the air between the apples. This moving air has less pushing power than the still air on the other sides of the apples.

Now place two large books about 10 cm apart on a table, and place a sheet of paper across them. Try to get the paper to float away by blowing under it. Can you do it? The answer is 'no' again, for the same reason as before. You will find that the paper droops down in the middle as you blow.

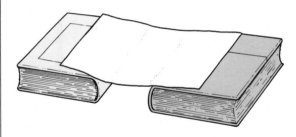

Lastly, try the same trick holding two sheets of paper in front of your face. Try to blow them apart. Once again, the moving air you blow between them should draw the sheets together rather than separate them.

The three-candle race

Fires will not burn without oxygen from the air. To keep a fire going, people sometimes blow on it or fan the flames to give it more air.

Here's a little experiment that shows how fire depends on air. You must ask an adult to watch you do this, as fires are very dangerous.

Fix three candles firmly to saucers or lids with modelling clay or something similar. Place them on a table in a safe place and light the candles. Cover one candle with a large jar, one with a small jar, and leave the last one open to the air.

Do you know which candle will burn for the longest time?

What is air made of?

Air is a mixture of gases. The chief gases that make up the air that we breathe are nitrogen (N) and oxygen (O).

When we breathe air into our lungs, the oxygen passes into the blood and helps to release energy from food. Used oxygen is breathed out as another gas, carbon dioxide.

Plants work in the opposite way. They use carbon dioxide (CO_2) and water to make their food, and they give out oxygen.

So the composition of the air is always changing. It also carries water vapour, which we'll forget for now. Do you think you could guess what the composition of dry air is? Is it (1) 57% O, 32% N, 11% CO_2, (2) 39% O, 39% N, 15% CO_2, 7% other gases, or (3) 78% N, 21% O, 1% other gases?

3 WATER AND ICE

When water gets very cold it freezes and becomes ice. It does this at a temperature we call the 'freezing point' of water. Water is a liquid and ice is a solid.

As water freezes and changes to ice, it expands and takes up more space. This makes ice lighter than water, so it floats in the water. About a ninth of the ice shows above the water. The rest of the ice floats below the surface.

Iced water

Float an ice cube in a glass of water, filling the water up to the top of the glass. What will happen when the ice melts? Will the glass overflow, will the water level sink or will it stay the same?

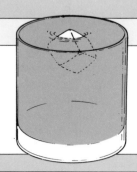

Burst pipes

Why do water pipes sometimes burst in very cold weather?

Cutting through ice

Here's a trick you can do with an ice cube. You need a bottle with a cork, two heavy forks and a piece of string or wire.

Balance the ice cube on top of the cork. Tie one fork to each end of the string and then hang the string over the ice cube. Now put the bottle, with the fork balanced over the ice cube, in the fridge. When you open the fridge again after a while, you will find that the string has passed through the ice without splitting it into two!

Do you know why this happens?

Floating and sinking

Density

Density is how heavy something is compared with its volume. You can work out the density of an object by dividing its weight in grams (g) by its volume in cubic centimetres (cc). The density of water is 1, because 1 cc of water weighs exactly 1 g. Is this an amazing coincidence, or do you think there is a reason for it?

If an object has a density greater than 1, it will sink in water. Objects with a density less than 1 will float.

A hollow metal ball weighs 250 g and has a volume of 500 cc. Will it sink or float in water? Look at the picture below. Can you guess which of the objects will sink in water and which will float?

The Plimsoll line

A ship floats at different levels, depending on its cargo and on the temperature and saltiness of the water. It floats lower in fresh water than in salt water, and lower in warm water than in cold water. A mark called the Plimsoll line shows the safe level for a fully loaded ship in various types of water.
Is it true that a ship can carry more cargo along a river in summer than in the sea in winter?

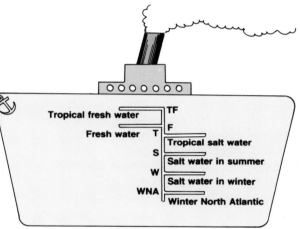

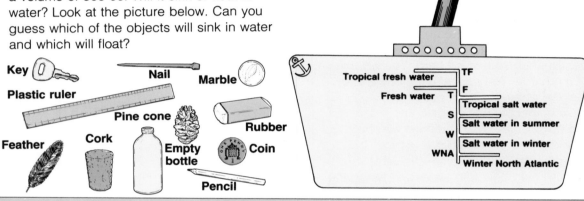

Key Nail Marble

Plastic ruler

Pine cone

Rubber

Feather Cork Empty bottle Coin

Pencil

What's wrong?

There are six things wrong with this picture. Can you spot them?

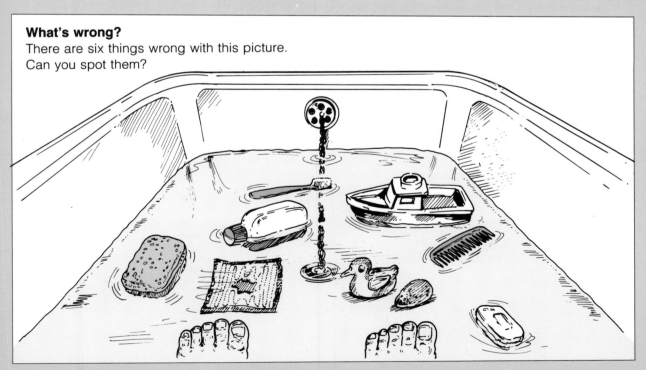

Water power

You can make water flow faster by squeezing it into a smaller space or by letting it fall from a height.

Find an empty plastic bottle, the squeezy kind used for washing-up liquid. Take off the cap, fill the bottle with water and then replace the cap. Hold the bottle over the sink or take it out of doors and try squeezing it gently. Then squeeze it hard. You will find that the harder you squeeze the bottle, the faster the water will spurt out.

Now empty the bottle again and make three holes in the side at different levels. Use a drawing pin or a nail to do this, but make sure that the holes are the same size. Now refill the bottle with water and watch the three jets of water as they spurt from the holes. Why does the lowest jet shoot out the farthest distance?

Underwater volcano

For this trick you will need a wide-rimmed jar and a small bottle. Fill the jar with cold water. Tie the string round the neck of the bottle and fill it with hot water. Add one or two drops of red food colouring or ink. Now lower the bottle into the jar and see what happens.

The red water rises up from the bottle just like a volcano. Do you know how this works?

Walking on water

If you look at water dripping slowly from a tap, you will see that the drops are almost perfectly round. This is because the surface of water is held together by a force called 'surface tension'. The water looks as if it has a thin, 'elastic' skin.

Some insects, such as pond skaters, can walk on water without sinking through the surface. They are very light, and the 'skin' of the surface is strong enough to support them.

Floating a needle

Here's a way to make metal float on water. All you need is a clean bowl, a fork and a needle. Fill the bowl with clean water. Rest the needle across the prongs of the fork and gently lower the fork onto the water, just breaking the surface. If you are careful, the needle will float off as you take the fork away.

Do you know why this works?

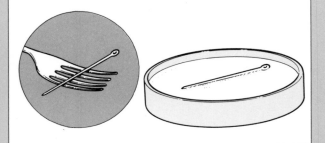

Skating on water

You've heard of water-skiing, but did you know that people also skate on water? It's not a trick, though. It's what happens when you skate on ice. The weight of a person through a skate's narrow blades puts great pressure on the ice. This melts it, and the layer of water helps the skates to glide smoothly over the ice. The water freezes again afterwards.

True or false?

Can you say which of the following statements are true or false?

(1) A peeled lemon floats on water.
(2) Nine-tenths of an iceberg shows above the sea's surface.
(3) Submarines dive under the sea by filling tanks inside the submarine with water.
(4) Ships float higher in salt water than in fresh water.
(5) Oil floats on water.

4 HOT AND COLD

All substances and objects are made up of atoms and molecules. These tiny particles, which are too small to be seen, are always on the move. The hotter the object, the faster they move and the more energy they have. Heat is a form of energy. The words 'hot' and 'cold' refer to the temperature of a substance or object.

Testing the temperature

'Hot' and 'cold' are relative. A person living in a northern city might describe an outdoor temperature of 25°C as 'hot', whereas a person living in a tropical desert would probably regard it as cool.

When you feel something to see if it is hot or cold, it depends on the temperature of your own skin. For example, you can put your foot in the sea or a swimming pool and think it is quite cold. But if you stay in the water for a while, it will feel warm.

You can show this with a simple experiment. Take two glasses of cold water and put some ice cubes in one of them. Stick your finger in this one for about a minute (if you can stand the cold!). Now put the same finger and the one next to it together in the other glass of water. The result is quite strange. What do you think you will feel?

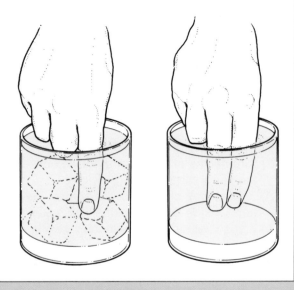

Making heat

Just as heat produces energy, energy can be turned back into heat. One way of doing this is by using friction, rubbing one object against another. Try rubbing your hands together. Can you feel them get warm? This is why you rub your hands together outdoors in cold weather. The more energy you use – that is, the harder and faster you rub – the hotter your hands will get. What happens when you rub two dry sticks together?

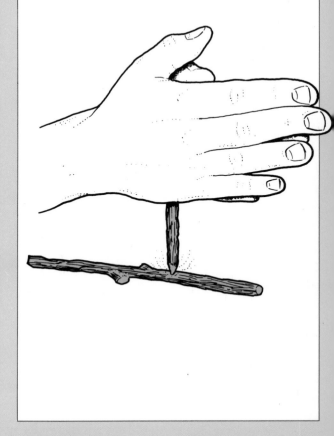

Making a thermometer

You can make a simple thermometer with a bottle, a clear tube such as a straw, a piece of plasticine and some coloured water.

Half fill the bottle with coloured water. Push the tube into the liquid, making sure it does not touch the bottom of the bottle, and seal the top with plasticine. Blow gently into the straw so that the liquid comes up just above the top of the bottle. Mark the straw at this point.

Stand the bottle in a sink and let the hot tap run along its side. What do you think happens?

Now run cold water over the side of the bottle. What do you expect to happen now?

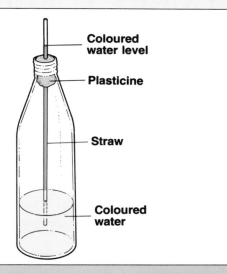

Coloured water level

Plasticine

Straw

Coloured water

'Hot' is lighter than 'cold'

Just as warm air is lighter than cold air, so warm water is lighter than cold water. You can prove this in your own bathtub!

Put some cold water in a plastic bottle, add some colouring, replace the top and shake to colour the water evenly. Place the bottle in a fridge for a few hours to make it even colder.

Half fill the bath with warm water and hold the bottle flat on the bottom. Carefully unscrew the top so that the cold, coloured water seeps out slowly.

Can you work out what happens to the coloured water?

15

5 TRICKY FORCES

When you throw a ball in the air, it falls back down to the ground. This happens because of a force called 'gravity'. Things are pulled together because of this force. The pull of the Earth's gravity is so strong that it keeps everything on its surface. Without gravity, everything on Earth would fly out into space.

Objects have weight because the Earth's gravity pulls on them. It's a force that acts on an object whether it is standing still or moving. Because of something called 'inertia', objects that are still do not want to move and those that are moving do not want to stop. You need force to overcome inertia, which comes from the Latin word for 'lazy'.

You can use gravity and inertia in all kinds of tricks and puzzles – even if you don't know what they are called!

Balance the see-saw

If you play on a see-saw with a friend of about the same size, you will balance each other. But what happens if one of you is much heavier than the other?

Try it by making a see-saw with a ruler and half a tube, using coins to balance. Cut a cardboard tube down the middle and use one piece. Place it flat side down and balance the ruler across it. Put one coin of the same size at each end. They will balance, because what we call the 'centre of gravity' is in the middle.

Now add a second coin to one end, making this lower. The problem is to balance the see-saw again without adding any more weights. Can you do it?

Tightrope walker

Problem – you have a small potato on the end of a cocktail stick: how do you balance the stick on a piece of string with the help of two forks? If you've ever seen a tightrope walker at a circus, you might work it out for yourself.

This is how it's done. Stretch the string (or wire or strong thread) very tightly, perhaps between two chairs. Make a notch in the end of the cocktail stick so that it fits comfortably on the 'tightrope'. Now stick the forks in the potato as shown in the illustration. You will find that the complete object – potato, stick and forks – balances because its centre of gravity is below the string.

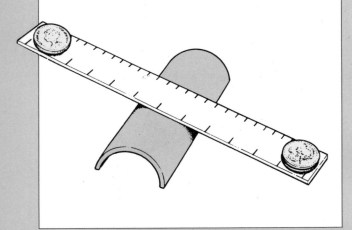

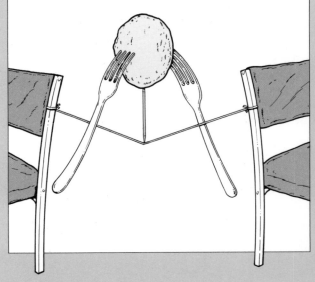

Lazy coin

Here's a neat little trick that uses the inertia of a heavy object – a coin. You might not think of a coin as a heavy object, but small objects can be heavy when compared with things made of lighter materials.

Place the coin on a piece of card that is resting on the edge of a glass. Flick the card as shown in the illustration and see what happens. The coin will drop into the glass. The reason is that it has too much inertia to be moved in this way and will just fall when the card is removed.

What do you think would happen if you used a matchstick instead of a coin? Now stand an empty matchbox on the card and balance a cooked egg on top. (Line the glass with tissue or a cloth to save it getting cracked.) Can you say what will happen when you flick the card away?

In a spin

When an object spins round, it makes what is called a 'centrifugal force', which pulls it outwards. You can feel this force if you attach a piece of string to a ball and whirl it round.

A good way to demonstrate centrifugal force is with water. Half fill a small bucket of water and take it outside. Try spinning it round with you in a circle quite quickly. You will find that centrifugal force will keep the water pressed against the bottom and the sides of the bucket even when you lift it above shoulder height.

Now swing it to and fro a couple of times and then up in the air and completely round. Even when the bucket is upside-down, the water will not come out.

6 SOUNDS GREAT

Sound travels in waves. All the sounds we hear are made by something vibrating. This makes the surrounding air vibrate, and the vibrations travel out in all directions. Sound also travels through liquids and solids.

The sounds we make when we speak or sing come from vibrations of the 'vocal chords' in our throat. Musical sounds are made by vibrating strings (violin), air (clarinet) or a drumskin, for example.

The faster something vibrates, the higher the sound it makes. We cannot hear all sounds. Some animals can hear much higher sounds than people can.

Which of these animals can hear the highest sounds: bat, cat, dog or dolphin?

Sounds through water and metal

Sound travels faster through liquids and even faster through solids. You can try this out for yourself.

Blow up a balloon and hold it next to your ear. Hold a ticking watch on the other side of the balloon. You can probably just hear it ticking. Now fill the balloon with water and try again. The ticking should be louder, because the sound is travelling faster. Do you know how much faster sound travels through water than through air?

Find a length of iron railings and ask a friend to tap on them at one end with a stick. If you are standing at the other end, you will hear the sound. Now put your ear close to the railings and repeat the experiment. What happens?

Guess the sound

You can make all kinds of sounds with different objects and materials by shaking, blowing, rustling or banging them. This makes a good game. Collect a number of different things together and set up a screen so that your friends can't see them. Then make sounds with the various materials and award a point to the person who is first to guess right each time. There's no end to the sounds you can make – rustle metal foil or tissue paper, blow through a straw, twang a rubber band, shake toothbrushes in a plastic mug, bang the edge of a cup with a spoon, and so on.

Music from bottles

You can make a musical note by blowing across the top of an empty bottle. This is because you are making the air in the bottle vibrate, as in a recorder or an organ.

If you change the amount of air in the bottle, it will make a different note, or musical sound. Try making your own bottle organ. Collect a number of bottles together and fill them with water to different heights, as in the illustration. By blowing across the tops in turn, you can make different notes, even play a tune.

Which bottles make the higher notes, the ones with most water or the ones with least?

Try tapping each bottle with a metal spoon. What happens now?

Music from straws

You can make a set of Pan pipes from a few straws and some corrugated cardboard. Push a straw through alternate openings in

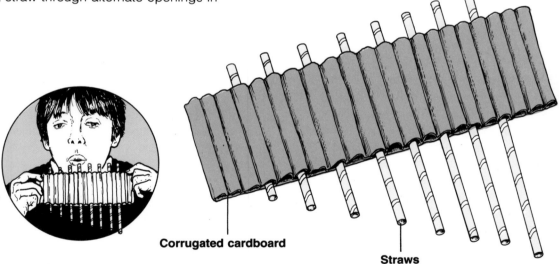

Corrugated cardboard

Straws

the cardboard. With a pair of scissors, cut each straw to a different length, the longest at one end going down to the shortest at the other. Make sure you have an even sloping line, as in the illustration.

To play your Pan pipes, blow across the tops of the straws. Which straw makes the highest note, the longest straw or the shortest?

7 POLES APART

Have you ever noticed how your hair sometimes crackles when you comb it on a dry day? Or perhaps you've had a mild electric shock after walking across a thick carpet and then touching a doorknob? These effects are due to 'static electricity'.

The atoms that make up everything have particles inside them with electric charges. The protons are positively charged (+) and the electrons negatively charged (−). If the atoms or molecules of a substance lose some electrons, they become positively charged. If they gain electrons, they become negatively charged. It is these charges that produce static electricity and also make things attract each other.

Bending water

You can make static electricity by rubbing things together. Rub a plastic comb several times on a woollen jumper and you'll be able to pick up tiny scraps of tissue paper with it. Do you know why?

Now 'charge' your comb in the same way and hold it next to a thin stream of water running from a tap. The water will bend towards the comb. Again, do you know why?

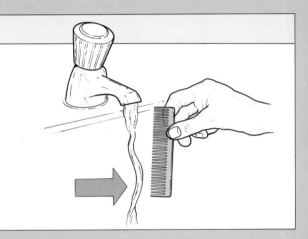

North and south poles

Most magnets are made from iron or steel. Some are long and straight, and are called 'bar magnets'. Others are horseshoe shaped. The parts at the ends of a magnet, where the magnetism is strongest, are called the north and south poles.   Can you guess why?

Magnets work like static electricity. Opposite poles attract. Like poles repel. Only certain metals can be magnetized, such as iron and nickel. When you approach a paper-clip, say, with the north pole of a magnet, you turn the paper-clip into a small magnet and its south pole is attracted to the north pole of the magnet. Can you explain the drawing near right?

You can compare the strengths of magnets by seeing how many paper-clips or pins they will pick up. Try picking them up in a bunch and also in a line. Try picking up a magnetized pin with another magnetized pin.

Here's a good trick. Pull a paper-clip out of a jar of water by sliding it up the side with a magnet (below right).

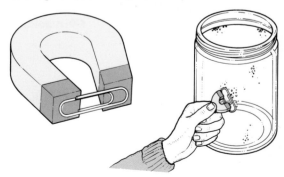

Invisible forces

The strange, invisible force that surrounds a magnet is not fully understood. You can see the pattern of this force by using iron filings. These are tiny bits filed off a piece of iron with a metal file.

Sprinkle the iron filings round a bar magnet. You will find that they cluster together in the place where the force is strongest. A lot stick to the ends of the magnet. Try it using two magnets, first with opposite poles close, then with like poles close. Another way to do this is to put a piece of paper over the magnets and then sprinkle the filings over the paper.

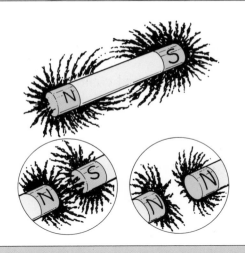

Opposite charges

Current electricity also works with opposite charges. Batteries have a positively charged end, or pole, and a negatively charged end. You can see the + and − marked on the battery.

The chemicals in a battery make electricity. The battery case is made of zinc metal, often covered with card and plastic or tin to prevent leaks. In the middle of the battery is a carbon rod, rather like a thick pencil lead. The space between the casing and the carbon rod is filled with a chemical paste.

When you join the two poles of a battery with a copper wire, current flows though the wire. Do you know what causes this electric current?

Brass cap

Carbon rod

Zinc casing

Chemical paste

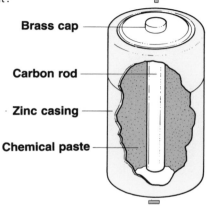

Spot the difference

The two pictures below are of the same corner of a kitchen. Some things have been removed in the lower picture. Can you say what these things have in common?

What's missing?

8 TIME AND CLOCKS

Once upon a time, people didn't have clocks. The only way they could tell the time was from day and night, the rising and setting of the sun each day. They knew the years from the changing seasons. Today, some clocks used by scientists are accurate to 1 second in 200,000 years. No excuse for them to be late!

Measuring time

The first units of time that were shorter than a day were hours. The ancient Babylonians, more than 4,000 years ago, used sundials to divide the day between sunrise and sunset into 12 equal parts, or hours.

On a sundial, the shadow of an object moves from one side to the other as the sun moves from east to west during the day.

You can make a sundial for yourself with a piece of stiff card and a piece of wood. If you want it to be accurate, you will need a protractor to measure angles and a compass to draw a semi-circle.

Cut out a triangle of card as marked in the drawing, with a strip underneath to fold over and stick to the wooden base. Keep the card upright with 'guy ropes' of cotton if necessary. On a sunny day, put your sundial on a flat place outside so that the triangle points north-south. Mark the position of the shadow that falls on the base every hour. You should find that the shadow travels the same distance round the semi-circle every hour.

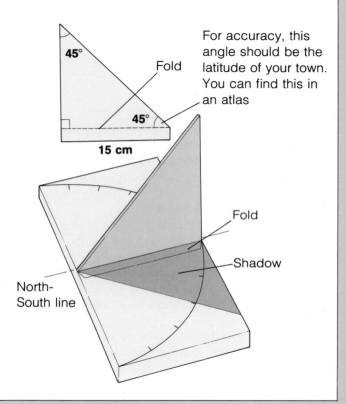

45°

Fold

For accuracy, this angle should be the latitude of your town. You can find this in an atlas

45°

15 cm

Fold

Shadow

North-South line

Digital time

Many watches and clocks of today do not have the traditional hands on a face, but show the time on a digital display. On a 12-hour clock, how many times a day are all the figures the same?

Atomic clocks

Split-seconds are important in sport. Track races are timed to hundredths of a second and swimming races to thousandths. But measuring time accurately is even more important in some sciences, where calculations might depend on microseconds (millionths of a second) or even less.

An atomic clock measures time by counting the number of vibrations made by atoms. Caesium atoms are used as a standard. They vibrate 9,192,631,770 times a second!

When is a year not a year?

Our year is the time it takes for the Earth to make one complete revolution of the Sun. Take out your calculator and see if you can work out how many seconds there are in a 365-day year.

The year on other planets is not the same. Mercury's year, for example, is only 88 Earth days, whereas Pluto's year is 248 Earth years. Venus orbits the Sun in 225 Earth days, but takes 243 Earth days to spin round once on its axis. Do you know what this means? It's day is longer than its year!

Armed with this information, see if you can work out this problem. A friendly alien from a distant planet lands on Earth. It meets two children playing in the forest. 'Can I play with you?', it asks, picking up the Earthly language without any trouble. 'Sure,' say the friends, who had just been watching ET on television. 'I'm eleven', says one of them, 'And I'm ten, but I'll be eleven tomorrow,' says the other. 'How old are you?' 'Well,' says the alien, 'I'm also ten, but I'll be twenty tomorrow'.

The children had a good laugh, but then they realized the alien wasn't joking. How come?

Reaction time

It takes time – a split-second – for us to react to a signal from the brain. At the start of a race, the sound of the gun is the signal for runners to go. Some get off before others because their brain sends messages to their muscles faster. They have what is called a quicker 'reaction time'.

You can test this with a friend. Take a 30-cm rule and hold it at the top so that the 30-cm mark is between and level with your friend's finger and thumb. When they are ready, they have to try to catch the rule between their finger and thumb as you drop it. The centimetre where they grasp the rule indicates their reaction time. Then get your friend to test you.

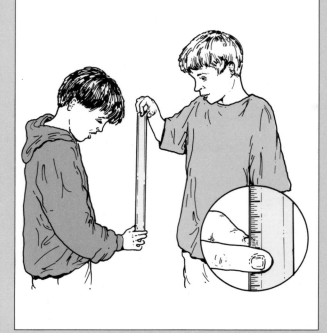

9 QUIRKS OF THE WEATHER

Weather is what happens in the atmosphere, the air that surrounds the earth. Heat from the sun causes great masses of air to move around. The land and the sea warm up during the day and then cool down at night. Water evaporates from the sea and forms clouds. Clouds might bring rain or storms. If it is cold enough, it might snow. In many places, weather is changing all the time. In others, it hardly changes at all. The type of weather a place has throughout the year is called its climate.

The effect of heat

The effect of the Sun's heat on land and water is different. Smooth, shiny surfaces reflect heat. Dull, roughened surfaces absorb it. You can try this out for yourself with a simple experiment.

You need two identical glass jars and a thermometer. (Take care when using a thermometer, because the mercury inside is poisonous.) Fill one jar with fairly dry soil and the other with water. Measure their temperatures with a thermometer, and put them on a sunny window ledge.

Measure their temperatures again after half an hour and then an hour. Obviously they will be warmer, but can you say whether one will be warmer than the other?

Now take both jars indoors, place them in a shady place and cover them with a black cloth. This will cool them down. Can you say which one cools down faster?

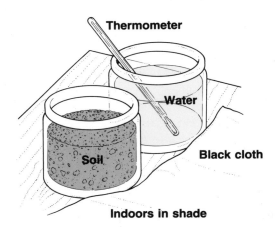

On windowsill in sun

Indoors in shade

Temperature scales

Most countries now use the Celsius (C) temperature scale, although Fahrenheit (F) is still used in places. The freezing point of water is 0°C or 32°F. Water boils at 100°C or 212°F. To convert Fahrenheit to Celsius, you first subtract 32, then divide by 9 and multiply by 5. To convert Celsius to Fahrenheit, you multiply by 9, divide by 5 and then add 32.

Can you change the following from one scale to the other: 77°F, 104°F, 5°C, −15°C? Which is lower, −40°C or −40°F ?

Measuring rain with a ruler

Rainfall is usually measured in millimetres (mm) of rain falling on a place – a city or region, perhaps – in a year or a particular month. Rain is measured with rain gauges, instruments that collect rain as it falls. A network of rain gauges placed about 15 km apart might be used to find the average rainfall of a region. An average of about 860 mm of rain and other precipitation (snow, sleet, etc) falls on the earth every year.

You can record the rainfall at your home by making a simple rain gauge. You need a large jam jar, a funnel and a piece of stiff plastic (like the packing around toys). The top of the funnel should measure across its top the same as the body of the jar. Cut it to size if necessary.

Choose an open place that is not shielded from the rain. Bury the jar up to its neck in the ground. Cut a small hole in the plastic sheet and jam the spout of the funnel into it. Then cover the top of the jar with the plastic so that the spout hangs down into it. Your rain gauge is now set up.

Each day or week, lift the jar out and measure the depth of the water in millimetres. This will be the rainfall for that day or week. Keep records and find out which are the rainier months of the year.

How does your rainfall compare with the wettest place on Earth. This is in South America – Tutunendo, in Colombia. Can you guess how much rain falls there every year? Is it 3,500 mm, 7,900 mm or 11,800 mm ?

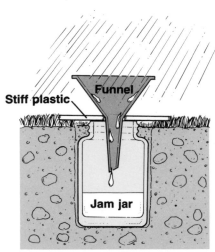

Rain-water collects in jar

Snowflakes

Did you know that every snowflake is different, but they all have six sides. Next time it snows, collect some on a piece of black cloth that has been left in the fridge or freezer and examine them with a magnifying glass.

Hailstones

Hailstones are raindrops that freeze into solid balls of ice. Most hailstones are about the size of small peas. But sometimes they get very big. The heaviest hailstones ever recorded fell on the Gopalganj district of Bangladesh in 1986, and killed nearly 100 people.

How much do you think they weighed: 100 g, 1 kg or 5 kg ?

Stormy weather

In a storm cloud, the moving air makes tiny water droplets and ice particles rub together. They become charged with static electricity. This builds up until the electricity jumps from cloud to cloud or to the ground as lightning. These giant flashes make the air so hot that it explodes with loud booms of thunder.

Because light travels so quickly, we see the flashes of lightning almost immediately. But sound travels more slowly, so we have to wait a few moments before we hear the thunder.

During a storm, wait until you see a flash of lightning, and start to count slowly in seconds ('one second, two seconds, three seconds ...' is a good way to count). For every count of 3, the storm is roughly 1 km away. Say you counted 15 seconds between a flash and a boom. How far away would the storm be?

Eye of the storm

A hurricane is a violent storm of whirling wind and rain. Hurricanes form over tropical oceans and grow in strength as they move. They can cause devastation if they reach land.

A hurricane might measure hundreds of kilometres across and take several hours to pass over a particular place. Yet you can be right in the middle of a hurricane and not realize it. How is that?

Odd one out

Winds are named according to the direction they blow from. A north-east wind, for example, blows from the north-east. In many parts of the world, at sea and over land, winds blow regularly from a particular direction. Old maps used to show winds as faces blowing out swirling clouds.

Local winds that blow at certain times of the year are often given names. See if you can guess which of the following is not the name of a wind: föhn, mistral, monsoon, convair, chinook, sirocco, harmattan.

Weather records

Driest

The driest parts of the world are the deserts. These may be sandy, stony, rocky or covered with dry, dusty soil. The world's driest place is the Atacama desert, in Chile. Rain is so scarce that it doesn't have an average annual rainfall. In some parts of the desert rain might not fall for a hundred or more years.

Are these statements true or false?

(1) Snow sometimes falls in the Sahara desert.

(2) The average annual precipitation (rain, snow, etc) over the Sahara is more than that on central Antarctica.

Coldest

The coldest place on earth is near the South Pole, in Antarctica, where temperatures average –58°C. Temperatures approaching –90°C have been recorded in Antarctica. The coldest place where people live is on the other side of the world, in Siberia. There, in the Russian village of Oymyakon, a temperature of –68°C was once recorded.

Scientists use alcohol thermometers or other special instruments to measure such low temperatures. Can you say why they can't use ordinary mercury thermometers?

Hottest

Claims to being the hottest place in the world come from areas as far apart as Ethiopia, in Africa, Death Valley, in North America, and Western Australia. It really depends on what is meant by 'hottest'.

Records are based on shade temperatures, and the hottest ever recorded was 58°C at Al'Aziziyah, Libya, in Africa. But the prize for the highest annual average must surely go to another African country, Ethiopia, where the temperature at Dallol taken over a six-year period averaged 34.4°C.

True or false: Summer temperatures of over 50°C are common in Death Valley, California?

10 SPACE AND SPACE TRAVEL

The Earth is a planet. It travels in a path, or 'orbit', around the Sun. There are eight other known planets. The Earth has one moon. Some planets have more than 10 moons. The Sun, the planets and their moons together make up the Solar System.

Since space travel began in the 1960s, people have explored parts of the Moon and sent spacecraft to study the planets. We study the stars with telescopes. Some spacecraft have left the Solar System on their way to the stars.

Planets quiz

(1) Which planet is nearest the Sun? (CLUE: Found in a thermometer)
(2) Which is the closest planet to Earth? (CLUE: Goddess of love)
(3) Which is known as the red planet? (CLUE: A chocolate bar)
(4) Which is the largest planet? (CLUE: King of the gods in ancient Rome)
(5) Which is the farthest known planet? (CLUE: A Walt Disney character)

Moon quiz

(1) How much does a person weighing 60 kilograms on Earth weigh on the Moon: 10 kg, 30 kg, 60 kg or 120 kg ?
(2) Why is the Moon's sky always dark, even during the Moon's day?
(3) What makes the Moon shine?
(4) What is an eclipse?
(5) On Earth, how many 'new moons' are there in a year: 1, 12, 13 or 52 ?

Sun quiz

(1) What is the Sun: a galaxy, a star or a red dwarf ?

(2) How hot is the Sun's surface: 550°C, 1500°C or 5500°C ?

(3) How many times would the Earth fit into the Sun: 1,400, 120,000 or 1,300,000 ?

(4) On average, the Sun is about 150 million km from Earth. How long does it take light from the Sun to reach us: 8 seconds, 8 minutes, 8 hours or 8 days ?

(5) How long does it take the Earth to make one complete revolution of the Sun: 1 week, 1 month or 1 year ?

The speed of light

We sometimes talk of something travelling at the speed of light, meaning it is going very fast. But the real speed of light is 300,000 km/h and nothing travels that fast. Even a supersonic airliner, faster than a bullet from a gun, doesn't go much more than about 2,000 km/h.

The speed of light does not mean very much on Earth, because light doesn't seem to take any time at all to travel. But when it comes to the great distances of space, the speed of light is very important.

Our nearest star, of course, is the Sun. It is our star, and its light takes just over 8 minutes to reach us. But what about the other stars? The nearest to our Solar System is a star called Proxima Centauri. How long do you think it takes light to reach us from this star: 4 days, 4 weeks, 4 months or 4 years?

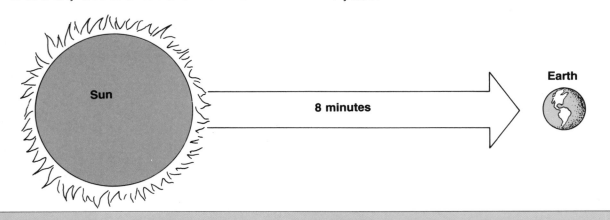

Sun — 8 minutes → Earth

Shapes in the sky

On a clear night, you can see about 3,000 stars in the sky without using binoculars or a telescope. Ancient peoples divided the sky into groups of stars called 'constellations'. They imagined the groups formed shapes in the sky and gave the constellations names of animals and other things. We still use these names today. The constellations have both Latin names and English names. Ursa Major, for example, is the Great Bear.

Can you say what constellations these are?

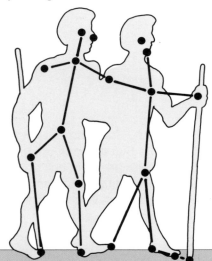
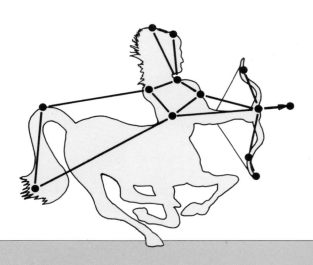

Galaxies

Most stars belong to groups called 'galaxies'. All the stars that we can see, even with the aid of the most powerful telescopes, are in our galaxy. It is called the Milky Way, because of its whitish appearance when we look towards the centre of it in the night sky.

How many stars do you think there are in the Milky Way: 10,000, 1 million, 10 million, 1,000 million or 100,000 million?

The most distant object that can be seen with the naked eye in the night sky is the Andromeda Galaxy. It looks like a tiny white oval shape, because of the billions of stars inside it. How far away, in light years, do you think Andromeda is: 500,000, 1 million or 2 million?

How long will the Sun shine?

Stars are 'born' out of great clouds of gas and dust in space. Drawn together by gravity, these particles form a globule which gets bigger and bigger. A star 'shines', giving out light and heat for a long time. But eventually, when all its 'fuel' is burnt out, it collapses and 'dies'.

Does this mean our Sun is going to die? Well yes, it will one day. But don't worry, it won't be for a long, long time. Can you say how long it will be before the Sun dies: 1,000 years, 10,000 years, 1 million years, 5,000 million years or a million million years.

Odd one out

In each of the groups on these pages, one thing does not belong. See if you can spot the 'odd one out'.

(1) Sirius
Saturn
Betelgeuse
Pollux
Proxima Centauri

(2) Taurus
Crux
Hercules
Aries
Gemini

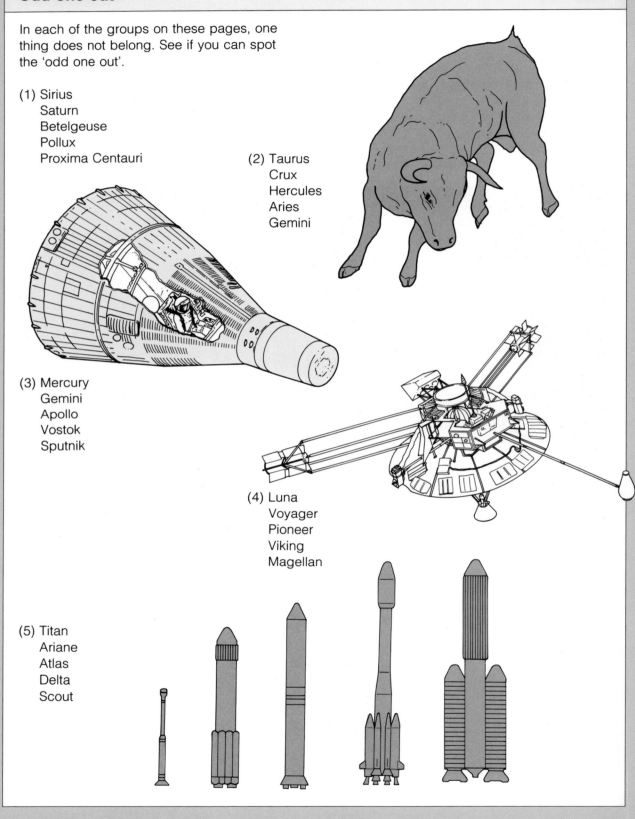

(3) Mercury
Gemini
Apollo
Vostok
Sputnik

(4) Luna
Voyager
Pioneer
Viking
Magellan

(5) Titan
Ariane
Atlas
Delta
Scout

Famous firsts in space

The brave astronauts and cosmonauts who are rocketed into space and orbit the Earth in their spacecraft are the explorers of the modern world. See if you can spot the famous pioneers of space travel in the groups on these pages.

(1) Who was the first person in space: John Glenn, John Young, Yuri Gagarin or Scott Carpenter?

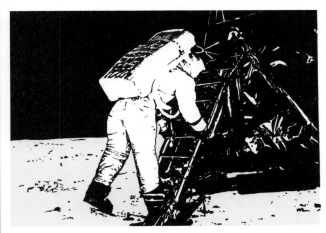

(2) Who was the first person on the Moon: Edwin Aldrin, Robert Crippen, Neil Armstrong or Bruce McCandless?

(3) Who was the first woman in space: Valentina Tereshkova or Sally Ride?

(4) Who was the first Briton in space: Patrick Moore, Isaac Newton, Heather Couper, Helen Sharman or Tim Mace?

ANSWERS

1 THE MIGHTY ATOM

It's elementary
Fe.

Solids, liquids and gases
Wood, steel, chocolate (unless it's melted!) and copper are solids. Milk and mercury are liquids. Carbon dioxide and air are gases.

Odd one out
(1) Water, a compound. The others are all elements.
(2) Bronze, a mixture of metals called an alloy. The others are also metals, but are elements.
(3) Sulphur is a non-metallic element. The others, also elements, are metals.
(4) Silicon, a solid. The others are gases.
(5) Dry ice, which is frozen carbon dioxide. The others are all forms of water.
(6) Aluminium, an element. The others are compounds.

2 ALL ABOUT AIR

Weighing air
The air in a large room would weigh as much as a person, about 70 kg!

Air to keep you warm
The warmest jar is the one that has the best protection, or 'insulation' as it is called, from the cold air. The first jar will probably be the warmest, because it has more air trapped between it and the cold air outside the wrapping. The third jar will also retain a lot of its heat because it also has a trapped layer of air to help in the insulation.

True – each layer of clothing traps a layer of warm air.

Air pressure
The pressure of the atmosphere is 1 kg per sq cm.

The three-candle race
The candle in the open will keep burning long after the ones in the jars have gone out, because they cannot continue to burn once they have used up all the air in the jars. The one in the smaller jar will go out first.

Now – make sure you put out the candle that wins the race.

What is air made of?
The answer is (3). Most of the 1% other gases is argon, so there is very little carbon dioxide in the air even though we are all breathing it out!

3 WATER AND ICE

Iced water
When the ice cube melts, the water level in the glass will stay about the same. This is because the water from the ice takes up less space than the ice itself.

Burst pipes
If the water inside the pipes is allowed to freeze, it expands to form ice, forcing the joints of the pipes apart or even splitting the pipes. This is why water pipes and tanks are 'lagged' with special materials to prevent the water inside them freezing.

Cutting through ice
Pressure can melt ice because it causes its temperature to rise. The pressure of the string or wire makes the ice melt just below it. Water forms under the string and it slides down through the ice. The ice freezes again just above the string.

Density
It is no coincidence that 1 cc of water weighs exactly 1 g – this is how the gram is defined in the metric system!

The hollow metal ball will float in water because its density is 250 divided by 500, which is 0.5, less than 1.

The objects in the picture that would sink in water are: key, plastic ruler, coin, marble, nail and rubber. The objects that would float are: pencil, feather, cork, empty bottle and pine cone.

The Plimsoll line
No, it is not true. River water is fresh, so a ship would be much lower in warm river water than in cold sea water, which is salty. So if it had a full cargo when setting out from a seaport in winter, it would sink if it then tried to sail up a warm river.

What's wrong?
The toy duck and the pumice stone should be floating. The toothbrush, soap and comb should have sunk. Did you get caught by the sixth wrong thing? The person in the bath has two left feet!

Water power
The water at the bottom is pushed down by all the water above it. This greater pressure forces it out faster and farther.

Underwater volcano
The hot water is lighter than the cold water, so it rises and floats to the top of the jar.

Floating a needle
Although the fork breaks the 'skin' on the surface of the water, it quickly forms again under the needle and stops it from sinking. If you look closely, you may be able to see the 'skin' bending under the weight of the needle. Another way of doing this is to support the needle on a piece of kitchen paper. As the paper absorbs water it will sink, leaving the needle to float, supported by the water's 'skin'.

True or false?
(1) False. A lemon floats on water only when it has the peel on, because air bubbles trapped in the peel make it less dense than water. (2) False. Only one-tenth of an iceberg shows above the water. (3) True. (4) True. Salt water is heavier than fresh water. (5) True. Oil is not as dense as water.

4 HOT AND COLD

Testing the temperature
The water feels warm to the finger that has been in the iced water, but cold to the other finger.

Making heat
Rubbing two dry sticks together makes enough heat to cause sparks to fly. This is how the cavemen used to start a fire. Scouts learn to start a fire with friction, too. The cavemen didn't have matches in those prehistoric times. Scouts are just forgetful.

Making a thermometer
The liquid in the tube will rise when you run hot water over the bottle, heating the water inside, and it will fall when you run the cold water. When the water heats up, it expands the air inside the bottle, pushing water up the tube, just as you did when you blew into the tube. In the same way, the air contracts when the water gets colder, and the liquid falls.

'Hot' is lighter than 'cold'
The cold, coloured water spreads out, but stays at the bottom of the bath. This is because it is heavier than the warm water in the bath.

5 TRICKY FORCES

Balance the see-saw
You move the pile of two coins closer to the middle of the ruler. You should find that the see-saw will balance when the two coins are halfway between the end and the centre of the ruler.

Lazy coin
Even a matchstick will have enough inertia to drop into the glass. When you try the trick with an egg on a matchbox, the egg should drop in but not the matchbox, which is being pressed to the card by the weight of the egg. The same thing would happen if you balanced a coin on top of a matchstick lying on the card. The coin would drop in but not the matchstick.

6 SOUNDS GREAT

The dolphin can hear the highest sounds, just higher than a bat. Cats can hear higher sounds than dogs – and both can hear much higher sounds than we can.

Sounds through water and metal
The speed of sound through water is about five times that through air.

The sound of the stick on the railing will be louder when you hear it through the iron, because it travels faster through a solid than through air.

Music from bottles
When you blow across the bottles, the air vibrates more quickly the less there is, so the bottles with most water make the highest notes.

When you tap the bottles, you make the water vibrate instead of the air. So the notes are the opposite way round, and the bottles with the least water make the highest notes.

Music from straws
The shortest straw makes the highest note.

7 POLES APART

Bending water
When you rub the comb on the jumper, you charge it with static electricity. The comb gains electrons and becomes negatively charged. When you put the comb near the pieces of tissue paper, the negative charge of the comb repels electrons on the paper to the side farther from the comb. As a result, the nearer side of the paper becomes positively charged and is attracted to the comb.

The stream of water is attracted to the comb in the same way.

North and south poles
They are so-called because one end is attracted to the earth's north pole and the other to the south. This is how a magnetic compass works. The poles are the magnetic poles of the earth, which acts like a huge magnet. They are not in exactly the same places as the earth's geographic poles.

The south pole of the paper-clip is attracted to the north pole of the magnet and vice versa.

Opposite charges
Moving electrons cause the current to flow. The electrons move in one direction and the current moves in the opposite direction.

Spot the difference
All the electric gadgets have been removed: cooker, toaster, clock, lights, microwave oven, kettle, washing machine, fridge, radio and mixer. Nowadays, we use electricity for so many things it's hard to imagine life without it, although not all of these gadgets or appliances have to run off electricity.

8 TIME AND CLOCKS

Digital time
12 times. The figures are the same 6 times every 12 hours: 1:11.11, 2:22.22, 3:33.33, 4:44.44, 5:55.55 and 11:11.11. Did you forget the last one?

When is a year not a year?
There are 31,536,000 seconds in a 365-day year ($60 \times 60 \times 24 \times 365$).

The alien came from a planet where the day was at least 10 times as long as the year.

9 QUIRKS OF THE WEATHER

The effect of heat
The soil will be warmer. It absorbs the heat faster than the 'shiny' water and so warms up more rapidly. When you place the jars indoors, you will find that the soil also cools down faster.

Temperature scales
77°F = 25°C, 104°F = 40°C, 5°C = 41°F, −15°C = 5°F. Neither, −40°C = −40°F.

Measuring rain with a ruler
The average annual rainfall for Tutunendo is just under 11,800 mm.

Hailstones
The hailstones weighed about 1 kg each.

Stormy weather
5 km.

Eye of the storm
Hurricanes rotate around a calm area called the 'eye', which may measure 30 km across. So if the eye passes over you, it might be calm for as much as an hour before the storm starts to rage again.

Odd one out
Convair.

Weather records

Driest: (1) True. Snow sometimes covers the mountain peaks of the Sahara, which rise as much as 3,000 metres above sea level. (2) True. The average annual rainfall over the Sahara is nearly 200 mm. Inland Antarctica is very dry, with 50 mm of snowfall a year. Some people call it a 'polar desert'.

Coldest: Mercury freezes at −39°C, so would be useless for measuring temperatures below this.

Hottest: True. Summer temperatures of 52°C are common in Death Valley. In August 1917, temperatures of 49°C or more were recorded on 43 consecutive days, and the highest temperature in the Western Hemisphere, 57°C, was reported there in July 1913.

10 SPACE AND SPACE TRAVEL

Planets quiz
(1) Mercury. (2) Venus. (3) Mars. (4) Jupiter. (5) Pluto.

Moon quiz
(1) 10 kg. (2) There is no atmosphere on the Moon to reflect or absorb the Sun's rays. It is the Earth's atmosphere that gives our sky its blue colour. (3) The light of the Moon is the reflected light from the Sun. (4) An eclipse of the Moon occurs when the Earth is between it and the Sun, blocking out the Sun's light. It looks like a shadow has been cast over the Moon's bright disc in the sky. An eclipse of the Sun is when the Moon blocks out the Sun's light from Earth. (5) 13. The Moon goes through 'phases' as Earth cuts out light from the Sun. At a full moon, we can see the whole Moon. As the Moon continues on its path round the Earth, we see less of it, until one night it is no longer there. Then we see the 'new Moon', a thin crescent shape which night by night grows into the full moon. There are 13 phases like this in a year.

Sun quiz
(1) The Sun is a star. (2) The temperature of the surface of the Sun is about 5500°C. (3) 1,300,000. (4) 8 minutes (and about 20 seconds). (5) 1 year.

The speed of light
It takes a little more than 4 years for light to reach us from the nearest star. Its distance from us is about 40 million million km. In fact, stars are so far away that astronomers measure distances in the time it takes light to reach us. Instead of saying Proxima Centauri is 40 million million km away, they say it is 4 light-years away.

Shapes in the sky
Gemini, the Twins (left), and Sagittarius, the Archer (right).

Galaxies
There are about 100,000 million stars in the Milky Way. Andromeda is 2 million light-years away.

How long will the Sun shine?
The Sun is about halfway through its life and will shine for another 5,000 million years.

Odd one out
(1) Saturn, a planet. The others are stars.
(2) Crux (the Southern cross) is the only one

of these constellations that cannot be seen from the Northern Hemisphere. (3) Sputnik, an unmanned spacecraft. The others are all manned. (4) Luna, a Soviet space probe. The others are all American. (5) Ariane, a European rocket. The others are all American.

Famous firsts in space

(1) Yuri Gagarin, the Soviet cosmonaut who was launched into orbit on 12 April 1961. (2) US astronaut Neil Armstrong, who stepped onto the Moon's surface on 20 July 1969. (3) Soviet cosmonaut Valentina Tereshkova, who made her first space flight in June 1963. Sally Ride was the first American woman in space, when she went up in the space shuttle Challenger in June 1983. (4) The first Briton in space was Helen Sharman, who flew in the Soviet Soyuz spacecraft on a mission to the space station Mir in May 1991.

MORE KINGFISHER PAPERBACKS
FOR YOU TO ENJOY

Superbook series:

WORD GAMES
ISBN 0 86272 199 7   £2.50

TRICKS AND PUZZLES
ISBN 0 86272 200 4   £2.50

GAMES TO MAKE AND PLAY
ISBN 0 86272 3159   £2.50

Let's Make Magic series:

CARD MAGIC
ISBN 086272 715 4   £2.50

EASY MAGIC
ISBN 086272 718 9   £2.50

MIND MAGIC
ISBN 086272 716 2   £2.50

MONEY MAGIC
ISBN 086272 717 0   £2.50

Kingfisher Books are available from most bookshops or by post from:

KINGFISHER CASH SALES
P.O. BOX 11
FALMOUTH
CORNWALL TR10 9EN

If you wish, you may fax your order to FAX No. 0326 376423. Please state your name and address and list the titles required.

Payments can be made as follows: Cheque, postal order (payable to Kingfisher Books) or by credit card Visa/Access (Mastercard), stating card number and expiry date, PLEASE DO NOT SEND CASH OR CURRENCY.

Please include with your payment the following amount for postage and packaging:

UK customers (including BFPO):
one book.. £1.00
second book ....plus £0.50
plus 30p each additional book
 to a maximum charge of £3.00
(7 books plus)

Overseas (including Eire):
one book.. £2.00
second book ....plus £1.00
plus 50p each additional book

While every effort is made to keep prices low, prices of books and postage/packing are subject to change without notice. Kingfisher Books reserves the right to show new retail prices on covers that may differ from those previously advertised here or elsewhere.